All Scripture references taken from the KJV of the Holy Bible, unless otherwise indicated.

Unstable As Water: Thou Shalt Not Excel

by Dr. Marlene Miles

Freshwater Press 2024

freshwaterpress9@gmail.com

ISBN: 978-1-965772-02-7

Paperback Version

Table of Contents

Unstable As Water:
Thou Shalt Not Excel

Freshwater

UNSTABLE as WATER

And Jacob called unto his sons, and said, Gather yourselves together, that I may tell you that which shall befall you in the last days.

Gather yourselves together, and hear, ye sons of Jacob; and hearken unto Israel your father.

Reuben, thou art my firstborn, my might, and the beginning of my strength, the excellency of dignity, and the excellency of power:

Unstable as water, thou shalt not excel; because thou wentest up to thy father's bed; then defiledst thou it: he went up to my couch.   (Genesis 49:1-4)

Levitical law states that a person shall not uncover thy father's nakedness. Isn't that what Ham did to Noah? Uncovered his nakedness? Believe what you will about that, but I see in the Bible that the nakedness of a man is his wife, his spouse, and in those days that would include his concubines.

The nakedness of thy father, or the nakedness of thy mother, shalt thou not uncover: she is thy mother; thou shalt not uncover her nakedness.

The nakedness of thy father's wife shalt thou not uncover: it is thy father's nakedness.

The nakedness of thy sister, the daughter of thy father, or daughter of thy mother, whether she be born at home, or born abroad, even their nakedness thou shalt not uncover.

The nakedness of thy son's daughter, or of thy daughter's daughter, even their nakedness thou shalt not uncover: for theirs is thine own nakedness.

> The nakedness of thy father's wife's daughter, begotten of thy father, she is thy sister, thou shalt not uncover her nakedness. (Leviticus 18: 7-11)

We are prewarned not to do any of these things in the Bible. FREAKY PEOPLE: **The freaky ideas you have are not your own thoughts.** They came straight from the pit of HELL because they are the very opposite of what God said. They have been sent to you to traumatize you, ritualize you, and destroy you. No Godly or sane person would ever desire to act them out, instead you should be repulsed by them. This is not the way to have a good time; these are acts that lead to evil initiation, ritualization, and eventually death.

> For the lips of a strange woman drop *as* an honeycomb, and her mouth *is* smoother than oil:

> But her end is bitter as wormwood, sharp as a two-edged sword.

7

Her feet go down to death; her steps take hold on hell. (Proverbs 5:3-5)

The *her* here is immorality--, the *spirit of immorality*. Even though this was written by men, for men, we all know that men can tempt women as well as the other way around.

Perverse things, perverse thoughts and perverse behaviors are not things to brag about; they are intended for your destruction and to send you to hell.

When something is the exact opposite of what God said NOT to do, then you know it is a hell thought, it is from the pit of hell and designed to pull you down to hell.

Jacob said to Reuben, "You shall not excel," and told him why. Why was he cursed not to excel? Jacob told him because Reuben is unstable. Obviously, stability is needed to excel. And Jacob further told Reuben how unstable he was--, *as unstable as water.* Moreover, Jacob told Reuben all this in front of everyone so it could not be misunderstood by anyone. He told him, *"Because you went up to my bed."*

Reuben delved into sexual sin. This is many times why people don't excel---, sexual sin. It could be, and *is* sin of any kind, but especially sexual sin.

On the matrimonial bed, no less; Reuben really had nerve, on the marriage bed that should be undefiled. In those days men such as Jacob who had two wives, before Rachel died, and also two concubines, which I consider side chicks that live in the same house whether the real wife or wives are okay with it or not, also slept on that bed. So why it was not already defiled could only be because men accepted this behavior in other men. Women may have as well--, at least on the surface.

And, if a woman tried that--, forget about it, she'd be stoned for adultery. If the other wives or sister wives did object to all this, they probably didn't say anything about it, else, they could be discarded and find themselves out of the house and out in the streets.

Jacob decried Reuben's behavior which amounted to **sexual immorality**, sexual impurity, ritual sex.

What's that?

Ritual sex is having relations with a person or people you are not married to regularly, and without repentance because it is either an accepted norm in the circles in which you travel, or you've done it so much and believe that nothing happened, so therefore you have decided it is ok. A person may be involved in ritual sex either because they are a *player*, or they think they are a player. They could be shacking up, that is, living with someone, or they believe they are in an *exclusive relationship* so therefore they believe they can do this. Where is that in the Bible? Where is any of that in the Bible?

Furthermore, *man of God*, if you are in sin, especially sexual sin, committing adultery and fornication **HOW** are you priesting and pastoring your own house, family and wife? How are you covering them, spiritually seeing that you yourself have stepped out from covering? From my Bible, I see in the Old Testament that the priest who was unfit to enter into the presence of God was dragged out dead because he didn't dare try to approach God as if he was living upright but hadn't. Now that may seem severe, but it is not up to me, it is up to God. God knows we are perfect, but we should be trying to walk upright before Him.

Repent and live. Those three words are for all of us.

Are you *playing* married because you plan to or think you may want to marry that person? Trying out the wares before you make the purchase? Every time anyone sins, they lose some glory or all their glory.

So Reuben, the firstborn of Jacob, a mighty man, a very rich man who came from the lines of Abraham and Isaac, both also very rich men, lost his inheritance. This was substantial. Reuben lost quite an honorable and large birthright because of a particularly heinous sexual sin. Not only that, he lost the blessing.

Nowadays most trust fund kids' foul behavior would be covered, winked at, looked over by their doting parents, but Jacob would have none of that. When speaking of losing glory, we understand that to be a spiritual transaction, but the manifestation of it in the natural is a dulling, dismissal, or loss of destiny. Things don't work out for you as they used to, or ultimately, should. You lose things, opportunities, divine connections. Reuben even lost glory in his own father's eyes. This parent didn't glance over this grievous sin; Jacob called it like it was.

Reuben became and was declared **unstable** by his dying father because of sexual sin.

Reuben was declared as *unstable as water* by his own father. In so doing we might say Jacob was keeping it 100, although it has been brought to my attention that Reuben did this thing many, many years prior, so why was dad just breaking it to him on his dying bed that he had been cut off? Still, we don't know that it was a surprise, perhaps the two had animosity between them and had been bickering about this for years.

Man!-- your firstborn, and you've got 12 sons---. What if the other 11 had followed the lead of Reuben? After all, firstborns are leaders and trendsetters in a family. Jacob had lost the one he really loved, Rachel, couldn't he at least have a woman of his own, or were his young, studly boys going to take his women? Levitical law says they shouldn't, but old men like Jacob might be insecure--, maybe *very* insecure.

This was considered a curse spoken over Reuben by Jacob, but didn't Reuben actually curse *himself*? Curses are built into sin.? Aren't certain curses automatically connected with certain sins? Would Reuben have been cursed automatically without Jacob speaking it to him, and especially in earshot of the rest of the entire family?

Sleeping with a married person is adultery, what does the Bible say about that? Should Jacob have forgiven this act by Reuben, and **could** he have forgiven him?

So is he who sleeps with another man's wife; **no one who touches her will go unpunished.** (Proverbs 6:29)

There are built in punishments for what Reuben did. Now when folks don't know any better and are quick to repent, forgiveness is usually forthcoming. Even Jesus asked the Father to forgive them for they know not what they do. But for hardened criminals, hardened sinners, and folks who do evil for the devilment of it, forgiveness is hard to get, if at all.

Did Reuben not realize what he was doing? Did he *accidentally* sleep with Jacob's concubine, Bilhah?

Oh please.

Not only that, this proclamation against Reuben was in front of **everyone**. It was not just a private conversation. Reuben had no defense, and as we see in the text, at that time he wasn't repenting to his dying father. There was no way anyone could say anything other than what happened, actually happened.

Plus, all the other people knew what Reuben had done; if Jacob had approved of it, or ignored it and blessed Reuben as if it hadn't happened, how do you think that would have set with the other children? Might they have lost respect for their father, also? It seems that Reuben didn't respect Jacob and that certainly is not a trend that Jacob would want established in the family.

The Firstborn Blessing

The blessing of the firstborn was huge, and Jacob knew that. Reuben's dad had taken the firstborn blessing of his own twin brother, Reuben's uncle Esau. Jacob and his mother, Rebecca had schemed to trick Isaac on his deathbed. I suppose Jacob had forgiven himself for his own underhanded acts, but he didn't forgive Reuben. Well, all the ways of a man are clean in his own eyes. (Proverbs 16:2A, James 1:8)

In Bible and patriarchal cultures, firstborn sons are given special privilege, honor and authority. The firstborn that opens the womb is special to God and to his parents. They are considered the first of a man's *strength*.

- The firstborn spends exclusive time with mother and father and are usually taught more things than the kids who come along after.

- There may be special blessings and impartations of knowledge and Wisdom to the firstborn that the others do not get.

- The firstborn is to be dedicated to God.

- It is said in the Bible over and again that Jesus was the Only Begotten of the Father and the Firstborn of Many Brethren.

- The firstborn can represent the family and father. Jesus certainly does.

- The firstborn, son especially gets double honor; they get more inheritance. In some cultures, they get all, and the other children get nothing.

- Often, they are the ones to administrate inheritance in the family after the passing of the parents, especially wealthy parents.

However, throughout the Bible, God does what He wants to do. God subverts that order whenever He chooses; He did it with Jacob and Esau. God will flip the script on the privilege and position of the firstborn son, for His own reasons.

Many times, He did it because the eldest son, as Reuben did, has disqualified himself. So, God may choose another because another family member may be more qualified. In the case of David, he was younger than all these upstanding brothers, but God chose David. Joseph was younger than 10 other brothers, but God chose Joseph. Joseph was way younger. And, as stated, Jacob was junior to Esau, but Jacob got the birthright.

And the Lord said unto her, Two nations are in thy womb, and two manner of people shall be separated from thy bowels; and the one people shall be stronger than the other people; and the elder shall serve the younger. (Genesis 25:23)

In patriarchal cultures, firstborn sons are given special authority and honor, double inheritance, along with the responsibility of **managing** their family's inheritance and becoming the patriarch of a family once the sitting patriarch dies.

Losing the firstborn is a particular punishment that we see in Exodus, spoken of in Psalms where the firstborn of Egypt were struck because of hard-hearted Pharaoh who would not let the Hebrews go.

And smote all the **firstborn** in Egypt; the chief of *their* strength in the tabernacles of Ham: (Psalms 78:51, Psalms 105:36, 135:8 and 136:10)

Firstborn sons are a big deal and are considered uniquely qualified to represent their fathers, purely because of their birth order.

Consider the things Jesus said, as He was Firstborn of Many Brethren, the Only Begotten of the Father. Jesus said, *I and My Father are One.*

God said, **Also I will make him** *my* **firstborn, higher than the kings of the earth.** (Psalm 89:27)

Jesus also said,

If you've seen Me, you've seen my Father. Jesus was not named, *Junior*, but a lot of proud dads expect their son to be a chip off the old block--, dad being the block. Dads should raise their son in the fear and admonition of the Lord, and not necessarily to be in the image and likeness of their biological father.

Jesus saith unto him, Have I been so long time with you, and yet hast thou not known me, Philip? he that hath seen me hath seen the Father; and how sayest thou then, Show us the Father? (John 14:9)

The Word says that Jesus was created in the image and likeness of God and thought it not robbery to be equal to God.

Who, being in the form of God, thought it not robbery to be equal with God: (Philippians 2:6)

Were we not, also created in the image and likeness of God?

And God said, Let us make man in our image, after our likeness: and let them have dominion over the fish of the sea, and over the fowl of the air, and over the cattle, and over all the earth, and

over every creeping thing that creepeth
upon the earth.

So God created man in his own image,
in the image of God created he him;
male and female created he them.
(Genesis 1:26-27)

When we were created, we were
in the image and likeness of God. Then
the Serpent walked in, and man fell;
therefore, our image and likeness took
on the image and likeness of the serpent,
or whatever demon we are now serving.
Therefore, our image and likeness have
to be rehabilitated after redemption and
salvation. Thank God that it is possible.

Jesus spoke, taught, and
exemplified the role of the *firstborn*
throughout His time here on Earth. He
fulfilled the Levitical statutes and
expectations of the firstborn as we have
outlined previously.

Paul equates the image of God
with being the firstborn of creation—

was fulfilled by Jesus but one that humanity is meant to live out as well. All humans, because of their responsibility to bear God's image, are meant to live as firstborn heirs over Creation.

Even so, know that the firstborn will have many spiritual battles and obstacles. It is obvious that Reuben wasn't doing a good job of meeting those expectations. After all, if you are steeped in sin, when do you have time to do spiritual warfare?

So, Reuben, the real firstborn of Jacob was passed over to receive the blessing of the **firstborn** because of *sexual sin* against God, because God had already said, ***Don't do that***, but as far as Jacob is concerned, Reuben sinned heinously against his father. Jacob took this seriously and didn't forgive.

The deathbed blessing is a serious thing; Reuben missed it. The deathbed mantle is also something to consider. Elisha asked God for a double portion of Elijah's mantle; is that something that we can do from our relatives? I consider the abundance of blessing and grace that a person who is passing on to Glory has not used or didn't get a chance to use, if their death is untimely. I consider their mantle; who will carry on in their stead? It is said that nature abhors a vacuum--, so if no one has stepped up or can step up to receive that mantle, that Grace, that time, shall we not ask the Father for that Grace and anointing, if we are related to or connected spiritually to that person? Elisha was not related to Elijah, but he was connected to him spiritually. This we only do if we know for certain WHERE that person got that Grace and those gifts. If it was not and is not from God, then you don't want it--, you can't trust that.

When You Used to be Against It

Saints of God I need us to rewind this recounting back to the time when in Jacob's family their only sister, Dinah went out one day and was captured and attacked also sexually--, raped by Hamor in Shechem. Her 10 brothers and their father were livid, and rightly so.

Afterward, Hamor decided that he loved Dinah and wanted to marry her and give money and valuables to Jacob, as if he was paying dowry or the bride price. The family rejected that. Instead, the boys devised a scheme. They tricked the men, attacked the town of Shechem, killed all the men. and captured the women and the children and brought them back home to be their slaves.

What was done to Dinah was an act of sexual depravity, sexual immorality, fornication, Illegal sex. It was also sin. And Reuben was 1000 percent against it--, that day.

How did Reuben forget that he was totally against illegal sex? How did he forget that he was against this sort of thing when he went up to his father's bed and went into Bilhah? I'll tell you how:

ALL the ways of a man are clean in his own eyes. (James 1:8)

We all need to check ourselves. And let the Holy Spirit bring us under conviction when we are WRONG, WRONG, WRONG. If we become as unstable as water, how can God bless us? If we become unstable as water, how can we excel? How can we succeed and prosper in the things of this life?

Reuben was the eldest, he was the one who had said, *Don't sell Joseph* after the boys had put Joseph in a pit in Dotham, many years earlier. Reuben had gone back to get Joseph out of the pit. But by that time, Reuben's younger brothers had already sold Joseph off as a slave to the Midianites.

Reuben had a heart then; Reuben had a conscience. What happened to Reuben? What had happened over the years to Reuben?

I used to think that Jacob's boys had no guilt and no conscience—that it had been seared or burned off. I thought they had no remorse, and just forgot about Joseph--- but folks, sin makes you stupid. Sin makes you stupid. Sin makes you more evil. Sin makes you dumb. Ephesians says that those who sin have their understanding darkened, which means they get dumber, and duller.

Sinning and then thinking you got away with it makes you prideful.

Guilt-consciousness, without repentance makes you CRAZY where you are trying to make what doesn't make sense, make sense. Over the years what they did to Joseph may have been gnawing at their consciences and eroding their souls, making them stupid, evil, hateful, suspicious of others, possibly.

This could have been what happened to Reuben.

It's Coming Back

In cultures where witchcraft abounds, if someone has the nerve to send a curse or evil arrows, unprovoked and unsolicited to another, **but that curse doesn't alight** –, because it can't. IT IS COMING BACK TO THE SENDER—automatically. This is kind of a-- *but they started it* thing. You are not instigating the curse, but you are also not letting it land on you or hurt you. You haven't started a war, but you are defending yourself. Yes, God is our defender, but we don't just sit on our haunches and get hit by evil arrows as if we are the target and the witches and warlocks are in target practice.

The Word says that he who digs a pit for another that they, themselves will fall into that pit. The Word says that he who rolls a stone, that stone will roll back on him. The Bible speaks of sowing and reaping—a man shall reap just what he sows. The Bible speaks of a man having what he says. Does not a witch or warlock *speak* the curse they are sending to their intended victim? Then, that man, especially if his intended victim is well protected spiritually, and that curse cannot alight on the intended victim, will he, himself have what he said.

You also are not ducking like Neo in the matrix to let it pass by you, because it could hurt someone else. You also are not letting it hover in your spiritual environment waiting for the best day and the best way to descend upon you with affliction, death, delay, poverty, or whatever it was sent to accomplish.

However, if the person who was to be cursed prays back to sender prayers. Oh, it's coming back on the sender.

So, the thing that a person sent to afflict another, kill another, hurt a person will come back on them. The sin of that witchcraft , and the sending of those evil arrows will affect the sender. Sin makes a person dumb, stupid, and causes them to hurt themselves.

Once that arrow comes back or the spell backfires, the first thing that generally happens is the person who sent the curse that didn't hit is they begin to go mad. They begin to go crazy. How many times have you heard a person say, *Oh, that crazy witch*. Over time, this craziness is bound to happen.

Witchcraft is sin, and unrepented sin can make a person mad. Madness, as in insanity, makes a person *very unstable--- unstable as water.*

Unrepentant sin makes a person as UNSTABLE AS WATER as Jacob connoted in Genesis 49.

Water, Water Everywhere

Water is the liquid we drink from glasses, bottles, and fountains, but in a moment under heavy or heated conditions, in uncontrolled violence, anger, and passion, water becomes **steam**. You've heard people say they need to blow off some steam, right? That means they are angry and are trying to get rid of the anger and calm themselves down. They are being hotheaded, so now it is as though the water that is in them is steam; they are steaming angry. We are 70 percent water and this has turned to steam. Anger and rage is coming out of them in random ways, in ways they didn't expect, and cannot control.

If left alone a person and their 70% water, without a Godly and human force, they may go into unforgiveness; they may become stuck. In this case water may become ice. These people are hardheaded and hardhearted. These types are not compassionate, and they just don't care about others. They are as cold as ice. When stuck, their emotions may freeze, and *water* becomes ice.

Water is unstable, it can become steam, water, ice --- water, steam, back to ice, and then turn back to water again, over and again repetitively. Humans are 70% water. Sometimes this is why they say we are subject to the moon and the tides and celestial bodies. The "water" in us if not properly ruled over can become unstable. Can you imagine if 70% of you is unstable, or stuck, or mean, or disobedient to God?

Water keeps transforming itself or letting outside forces transform it, over and again. Similarly, if a soul is not well-ordered, the same can happen—so much variableness. Eventually it can evaporate and then there is nothing there at all. Nothing but dryness--, just dust and dirt. We need water for life and we need stability for life and success. Without it, we will be just the dust and dirt that we are made of.

Saints of God, what will it be today? Hot or Cold? Steam or Ice? Can't it just be water--, stable water? You've heard it said some have passions that run hot and cold, but God said that He prefers you be hot **OR** Cold; not both. Be one or the other, not running the gamut trying to be both. Plus, when you are hot and cold that is lukewarm, and what actually is that? Something God will spew out of His mouth.

Every good gift and every perfect gift is from above, and cometh down from the Father of lights, with whom is no variableness, neither shadow of turning (James 1:17-18)

Be Stable

We want to be stable in our lives. We want to excel; we want to achieve and accomplish great things in this life. Well, how do we do that? The key to being stable is spiritual stability. We want the good things in life; we want the abundant life. We want to experience the abundant life that God has planned for us--, plans of peace and good success, and an expected end and live in health, with prosperity. We want to live in joy as well, enjoy the other Fruits of the Spirit.

We need to exhibit and share the Fruits of the Spirit, but we need to live in an overflow where we *receive* of the fruits of the Spirit, as well. Those fruit are hard to come by in survival or warlike conditions.

We need to be steadfast. Philippians 4:1 admonishes us to stand and be steadfast. We must have a strong spirit man so when something evil suddenly takes place in life, they don't fall apart. Instead, we withstand it; we don't get tossed about, back and forth by winds of doctrine.

Doctrine--, yeah, we study the Word of God so when something is coming against us that is not the Word of God, we must know and be able to resist it. We, therefore, endeavor to know the Word of God and to yield to the Word so it can change and strengthen us.

We want stability.

There is a certain glory on stability. Where there is glory, God will find you. Where God is there are blessings. Where there is glory, blessings will find you. There must be stability for blessings to locate you.

Financial Stability

Financial stability is a result of all the other parts of your life being stable. The rest of your life has to be right, or you could achieve or acquire what you believe is enough, financially, but will you keep it? If you are not able to keep it, how will you maintain anything? How will you maintain your life, your career, your family, your home, your marriage? People are not patient like God; they may not put up with your instability for years and years. Unlike God, they may just bolt on you.

You are more likely to achieve financial stability if you are not having ritual sex and *playing* people sexually all over the place. Virtual sex is ritual sex. Masturbation is ritual sex. Perverse sex is still sin and it is worse than the conventional stuff, and it is ritual sex. Ritual sex, which can stem from an overwhelming urge and lust, services the idolatrous sex altar, whether you realize it or not. Yes, it is a form of idolatry.

Perhaps you are not having illegal sex, but you've decided you don't want to burn with lust, so you've gotten married? Well, good. That can lead to financial stability. The man who finds a wife finds a good thing and obtains the favor from the Lord. There is favor in stability and there are blessings in cleaving to your own spouse.

The favor of the Lord is life. (Psalms 30)

Argue against this all you want but haven't you noticed that the boring people who got married, stayed married and built a family and a life are **stable**? Haven't you noticed that those who are out here running the streets, if they even make it to live out half their days, are somehow always at a deficit in some aspect of their life? Haven't you noticed that they move a lot? They may move from house to house, or town to town and often end up living in some downtrodden place when it is all said and done. They've spent their money on the good life, on partying, men have spent their money on women and wine. Because of no discernment or desperation, some unstable, silly women may have been duped out of their money by men, if these women even worked at all.

He who loves pleasure *will be* a poor man;
He who loves wine and oil will not be rich. (Proverbs 21:17)

She's back, the *spirit of immorality*, and this is what will happen if you serve at her altar for a long time, or possibly at all. Many have lost all for worshipping at the wrong altar even only once.

Remove thy way far from her, and come not nigh the door of her house:

Lest thou give thine honour unto others, and thy years unto the cruel:

Lest strangers be filled with thy wealth; and thy labours *be* in the house of a stranger; (Proverbs 5:8-10)

Being married leads to stability. Enjoying your own spouse leads to stability. There is favor and there are blessings in **stability**. You may say that stability leads to marriage. Okay, that makes sense. If you see *players* out here in these streets, you pretty much know they are not stable.

When you cleave to your spouse you unite as one. Where the people are ONE there God commands the blessing.

The World Is Not Your Friend

The world is not your friend. We are not to be friends with the world. The world says, *Be a player. Play around, have fun and don't get married.* The world will send you to hell, broke, busted and disgusted. There is a superlative and superior blessing in getting married and staying married, cleaving and being stable, and enjoying the spouse of your youth.

The world will make you unstable.

How so?

- What is the latest trend?
- What's everybody doing?
- What's the latest slang?
- What is the latest fashion?
- What is the latest fad?

Following after what everyone else is doing may make you throw in your gold with everyone who voted on it to build a golden calf. Following after fads and trends will make you unstable.

Women: what are you willing to become to get his attention because you do want to get married? Who are you willing to be to show him that you are wifey material or his type? Don't make yourself unstable by making yourself over and over from week to week or month to month. trying to attract, impress, please or keep the next one and the next one.

Ask God where your divine connection is, be there, go there, meet that person. Be yourself.

- Men what gym do you go to so you can be her *spec*?
- What are you willing to do to have enough money to get the trophy wife that you want?
- Do you want to impress your bruh's with the woman you can *pull*, more than you want to please God by getting into your correct, kingdom marriage?

You need to get the wife that God says for you to have; that's the wife and marriage that will prosper you and lead you to your destiny. Ask God. Pray and ask, *"Where is my divine connection, who is it? When is it? How do I get there and be sure that is where I should be? How do I prepare and when am I ready for that?"*

Instability--, changing to be like everyone else, changing to fit in so you won't get left behind. That may be exactly what will get you left behind, being like everyone else. God has created you as a masterpiece, a designer original, if you are like everyone else, your divine connection may pass you over, like looking in a crowd for Waldo.

Next year a new season of trends, fads and new fashion begins—who are you going to be next year at this time? That is instability, that is following after vain persons. These people who design and program all this stuff are not saved, are they? Predominantly hair, fashion, beauty, and the movie and music industries are run by the evil marine kingdom.

Changing yourself like a chameleon; why does your hair have to be green today and purple tomorrow? Don't be tossed about by the world.

Their doctrine is broadly cast out to the world to see who will buy it and buy into it. It is **broadcast** by the latest ads online, on TV and the latest music videos.

Broad is the way to destruction.

Enter ye in at the
strait gate: for wide *is* the
gate, and **broad** *is* the way, that
leadeth to destruction, and many there
be which go in thereat: (Matthew 7:13)

Do you think you exhibit stability? Are you walking upright before the Lord? Through the Strait Gate?

Jesus Is Stable

Jesus is the **same** yesterday, today, forever. (Hebrews 13:8)

That sameness exemplifies stability.

Sameness is not boring- it is dependability.

Sameness is not boring – it is sanity.

Sameness is not boring – it is LOVE.

Sameness is the way of Jesus, and it is not the way of the world. When something changes a lot, or often, or to the extreme, it is to get your attention. Moving objects. So many carrots dangled before people. Her hair is blue today and pink tomorrow—that is usually to get someone's attention. His car is a Toyota today and a Ferrari tomorrow—to get the attention of the ladies. Even putting something on sale, changing the price is to get the buyer's attention.

> Jesus is the **same** yesterday, today, forever. (Hebrews 13:8)

We all had better be thankful that God is dependable, reliable, and stable. It is why we are alive.

> For I am the Lord, I change not; therefore ye sons of Jacob are not consumed. (Malachi 3:6)

Folks, the reason the world is like that, changeable, mercurial, and flip is because there are billions of people in the world and the devil is broadcasting, that is casting out broadly--, throwing stuff up against the wall to see what will stick. The devil is testing to see what trick or trap will attract and trap you. He keeps trying things until you fall for one of his tactics--, or more than one.

Jesus is not trying all kinds of crazy stuff from moment to moment. Nope; Jesus is the same. He is not unstable; He is the same.

Back in the day when they would ask, What would Jesus do? I'll tell you what Jesus would do: He would **STAY THE SAME**. Jesus would remain stable. He would stand, and stand, therefore. Jesus is the same yesterday, today, and forever.

Jesus would say, IT IS WRITTEN. Saints of God, IF IT IS **WRITTEN** THAT MEANS IT IS THE SAME AS WHEN IT WAS WRITTEN.

Sameness is comfort.

Sameness is peace, where instability is stress.

Sameness and stability build, instability tears down.

Sameness is PROTECTION.

Sameness is your defense.

That sameness in Christ, not the sameness of tradition and because grandma and grandpa did it this way— unless they were in Christ, and fully *in*.

Even when God says He's going to do a new thing, and He does say that in the Book of Isaiah. It is not a thing of instability, like He is trying out something just to see what will happen. God doesn't promote fads or flukes. God's new thing is a new improved and better, **STABLE** thing. God's *new thing* is a God-thing to counter and or eradicate the world's thing that you've either been doing or have gotten yourself caught up in. God's new thing in the New Testament was the Better Blood and Jesus Christ. God's new thing is to get you out of the devil's old thing that may have ensnared you, trapped you, and is holding you captive.

Load Bearing

God's new thing is dependable, it is reliable, it is sound, and it can *keep* you. You can rely on it; you can stand on it. And stand, therefore.

Erratic, irrational, unstable people are not dependable. They are not seen as strong and cannot be leaned on in times of trouble. A broken tooth or a foot out of joint--, you can't put weight or force on either of those.

You cannot put weight on anything unstable. You can't even lean on an unstable person.

The Bible says that the Lord daily loads us with tender mercies. Saints, if we are unstable, how will we even take that loading? Those are blessings; shall we be able to accept and retain them?

No, not in instabiity.

That is why unstable people don't get things, such as blessings, inheritance, grace, anointing. God is not wasteful and will not pour out blessings unless you are ready and can receive and retain them.

Saints, there is a **weight** to the Glory of God. Seriously, it is heavy. How many have ever felt or had the burden of the Lord? It has a weight to it, even though it is spiritual. The unstable cannot accept or bear that weight. We must be both stable and steady to carry the weight of God's glory, as well carry the glory of man, as well, carry the anointing of God.

Location Stability

Location stability opposes and defeats the *vagabond spirit*. The Word speaks of people who can't keep their feet at home; that is the *vagabond spirit* working against their lives. Where people are together and united, that is where God commands the blessings. when the people *is* one there God commands the blessing. If you are not where you are supposed to be, and fitly joined to the people you are supposed to be joined with, you may miss your blessings.

Proverbs 7 speaks of the loud, adulterous woman, but women are not the only adulterous types. We all know too well of the man who wants to get out of the house who will pick a fight so he can leave. Evil *spirits* are in full effect in that man and purpose to destroy that marriage.

(She is unruly and defiant, her feet never stay at home; (Proverbs7:11)

People are blessed individually. Marriages are blessed because of the unity. As well, there are corporate blessings, where whole congregations are blessed because the people have become one. Of course, that means *one* in a Godly sense, not just one because they all have voted and decided on what sin they will all approve of, or look over.

God came down into the Garden and said, ***Adam, where are you?***

If you can be where God can find you, God will bless you there. There is no place where God can't find you; but you need to be in a Godly place and most often be found *doing*.

Doing what?

Well, not sinning for sure. God is not going to bless you in an illegal bed working on, and adding iniquity to your *thou shalt not excel curse*. Selah.

Be found doing. Jesus mentions that we should *occupy* until He returns. Who are you to God? Are you a teacher, a preacher, a prophet? Be found doing that, or at least preparing to do it if you haven't started yet. Be found *doing*.

Adam and Eve were in and dressing the Garden, that is what they were told to do and assigned to do. Can we not see that when they sinned, they now became preoccupied with the fall out of sin. What they were originally doing changed; they changed occupations. Now they are pre-occupied with either sinning or trying to get out of trouble from having sinned or hiding from God to avoid the trouble caused by the sin.

They aren't dressing the Garden anymore; now they are concerned with dressing themselves.

We don't see in the Bible that Eve kept on eating *apples--,* but folks, if Reuben lost the birthright and got kicked out of the blessing because of sexual sin, what do you think Eve actually **did** to get them kicked out of the Garden? Come on, saints of God, why do we still grow apples and eat apples if the Tree of the Knowledge of Good and Evil grew *apples*, and it is sin to eat them?

For those who are somewhat or very versed in occultic rituals, why is **sex** and especially perverse sex such a predominant act in so many evil rituals?

Why doesn't the occultist JUST GIVE HIS VICTIM AN **APPLE** TO EAT TO SEAL THE DEAL, to ratify and formalize the evil covenant?

Nope--, no apples, it is most often **sex**, and it is perverse and *very perverse* sex that seals many devil deals.

The occult is the Tree of the Knowledge of Good and evil, or the epitome of it. The devil planted that tree and God said stay away from it. Those who don't certainly know evil in a deep and intimate way. Evil sex seals it.

The victim may believe or think they are aware and willing to commit the sex act, but they could be duped, drunk, or drugged and tricked. The deal is still sealed if your **body** did the act, or if the act was done to you, whether you agreed to it or not. Whether you knew what you were agreeing to, or not.

Lord, help us all.

There is no where you can go and God can't find you, but He will not always bless you where He finds you. He won't if you are found in an evil place, not in an illegal bed, especially.

Nope. Well, except to bring you under conviction by the Holy Spirit so you can stop that behavior, get out of there, and repent.

You must be steadfast, steady, and stable. What you read in the Bible, and you agree to is what you believe in. Be steadfast in what you know and what you believe in; if you know better, do better. Don't be blinded to the fact that just because *you* are doing it or **want** to do it that it is not sin. All the ways of a man are clean in his own eyes--, just because you want to do the deed, you **want** to sin, doesn't make it right.

Remember sin is demon-inspired and demon assisted. God made man in His own image and likeness; we were not made to sin, to like sin, pursue sin, or want to sin--, that is as we were formed by God. But over time, sin markers have been placed in our foundations and it is natural for too many. David said he was conceived in sin and shaped in iniquity. God, on the other hand FORMED us, and we were made perfect, and we were made to worship Him and not demons, devils, and idol *gods*.

Do not hate sin on Monday but by Friday you *forget* that you hate it because you want to do something that you shouldn't be doing this weekend. Do not forget, like Reuben, that you hate illegal sex because somebody has been talking you into a "date" on Friday via late night phone calls Tuesday through Thursday. Talk is cheap but what you may be talked into is expensive. All that hot air is demon speak; it is as winds of doctrine in attempts to get you to *change* what you know, and what you believe in. After that, the expectation is that you *act* on your new beliefs, or misbehave on your suspended beliefs.

Brainwashing, wiping your brain clean of decent thoughts is as good as an occultic person wants it. They want your BODY--, to get your body to do evil stuff. In this way demons use your living, physical, human body to do evil that they really want to do, if they had bodies.

But God expects people to remain steady and stable; that is why He blesses what He formed and how He formed it with the expectation that the body will perform the way it was designed.

People who hide are guilty, scared, or doing something sneaky, and or diabolical. They are sinning or have recently sinned. The hallmark of the kingdom of darkness is that they embrace the darkness. They are occultic, they are hidden and propose to hide from others to do their rituals, spells, and dastardly deeds.

Occupy until Jesus returns is impossible if you are sinning. Adam and Eve stopped their *occupying* and turned their thoughts on what to wear. Being consistent and stable is impossible if you are sinning. Following after the world and being worldly is sin.

Glory Supports the Blessing

Chances are when you are running from pillar to post and place to place and house to house that you are not yourself, do not look like yourself, you're not being yourself. Many change up to behave or misbehave like the people that they are with.

When all that changing moves into sin--, any kind of sin, but especially sexual sin, you have either given your glory away, or it has been stolen from you while you were in the throes of passion, or whatever that was that you did in that illegal place, and on that illegal bed, if there was a bed. People do all sorts of things in all sorts of places that I don't need to describe here.

The Serpent came and there was sin, that is how and when he took Adam and Eve's GLORY.

God came down into the Garden, but that day He couldn't find them. God was looking for them. As Adam and Eve were supposed to be dressing the Garden because darkness and formlessness had fallen on the Earth after God had created it, can we not reason that once Adam and Eve's glory was gone, they looked just like the world they were in--, so God had to look for them? The beauty and the form that God had created in them was gone and they were dull, and lackluster, and stupid--, like everyone else?

Reuben sinned sexually. Sexual sin is about the best way to create a covenant. It is the easiest way for the devil to send in all kinds of demons. Sexual sin is the easiest way for an agent--, spiritual or human, to steal another person's glory or for that person to lose glory.

Reuben had a mighty inheritance coming to him, no doubt. Come on, his father was a prince and that was proclaimed by God. How could Reuben's anticipated inheritance be anything other than exceptional?

Reuben had lost his glory, and that glory was needed to support what would have been placed in his stewardship. He just didn't have a way to bear that inheritance, and most importantly then and even now—to keep it.

How many times have you heard of or seen trust fund kids get all kinds of crazy wealth and lose it in no time flat? That is a sign that they had no glory and were not worthy of that inheritance.

Chances are very good that the doting parents *covered* for that child who as we see in the natural had no character. But really, in the spiritual realms that child had no glory—it was lost, it was gone. But the parents pretended that their kid was normal, was okay, or they hoped their kid would change. Why they thought that, I'm not sure. They've been giving the child everything all of their lives and none of that built character, so why would giving them everything as inheritance, in a last will and testament be character-building?

As soon as that sin happened in the Garden Adam and Eve were evicted, kicked out of the Garden, as if God, who was providing their housing, divorced *them*. One of the first things that goes often in a divorce is the house you live in. Adam and Eve got divorced from

God who was providing their house, so they got kicked out.

Location stability depends on your relationship with God. You can go through a divorce and never lose your house or your ability to remain in the house you call home. Distancing yourself from sin, be all in Christ, and He will always provide for you.

Emotional & Mental Stability

Emotional and mental stability means that your spirit man is running your soul, and your soul is not running your spirit man. Your soul, especially not your emotions are not running your life. Emotions can toss you about all day every day.

Your mind is full of thoughts that come from many *voices* in the natural and from the spiritual world. You may not hear them audibly from the spirit, but you receive them as suggestions, ideas, nudges, influences. If you are stable, you throw out the ones that are not of God because you are diametrically opposed to them and or you find them evil, ignorant, stupid, or ridiculous.

If Jesus is the LORD of your life, and you have the Holy Spirit, then the Holy Spirit ministers to your spirit man and then your spirit man runs your life and that leads to stability. Your soul is not to run your life regarding emotional stability.

When it comes to mental stability, when you are in Christ, you think differently. When you access the Mind of Christ and receive the Spirit of Wisdom, for example, then you think on these things.

Finally, brethren, whatsoever things are true, whatsoever things are honest, whatsoever things are just, whatsoever things are pure, whatsoever things are lovely, whatsoever things are of good report; if there be any virtue, and if

there be any praise, think on these
things. (Philippians 4:8)

If you can sin while thinking on
any of those above things, then you
might have a very perverse mind, and all
the wrong *spirits* within you.

We think on the things the Bible
says to think on and not every crazy
imagination presented to you by the
devil and his representatives. We don't
think on things that some unsaved
person says. Or something you saw on
TV or in a movie. Don't listen to those
suggestions; apply the Word of God to
them immediately. This still takes
spiritual acumen, to discern if the Word
is of God, the thought lines up with the
Word, and or the person speaking is a
trusted mouthpiece of God.

The Serpent still speaks, and
often from pulpits. They may say they
are of God. They may be introduced by
someone who says they are of God. A

false, pastor, prophet, apostle, or teacher may be surrounded by people that you know or believe are of God. They may be wearing very nice suits and fancy jewelry, but are they of Jehovah God?

Discern every *spirit*.

What does unstable as water mean? Going from water to steam back to water and then to ice in a moment--, being curiously and quickly changeable.

"Unstable as water, thou shalt not excel." Did Jacob mean emotionally? Did he mean spiritually? Did he mean mentally? Did he mean in every way? We don't know for sure, but we do know that Reuben lost his birthright and his leadership position due to his instability. Reuben lost his ability or his blessing to excel when he sinned sexually; that is the sin which affected Reuben's stability. That is either when he became completely unstable, or it was the start of Reuben becoming

unstable. Jacob may have summarized that by knowing that Reuben knew better and had in the past probably stated that he knew better, but when and arrow of instability hit his mind, spiritually speaking, Reuben changed his own Godly, ethical, moral, and decency policy and slept with his father's concubine on his father's bed. Reuben got that idea from somewhere, and that idea was ungodly. But he acted out the transgression anyway.

For their heart was not **steadfast** with Him,
Nor were they faithful in His covenant.
(Psalm 78:37)

One must be steadfast and determined to keep the Word of God because temptations and attacks will come. The unstable are not steadfast.

Do You Hate Me?

Reuben, do you love your own natural father, or do you hate him? Sleeping with another person's spouse – a person that you know, related to them or not, means that you **hate** that person. Sleeping with another person's spouse means you think you've won over them--, you've conquered that person. When those 10 sons of Jacob and all the men that were with them bought all those women back from Shechem after they had burned the town, what do you think those men were planning to do with or *to* those women? In the minds of the victors, they are saying they have conquered the men of Shechem--, they've won. They've won because now they have the women. They are also thinking that these women are property so they can do with them as they please.

Having illegal or ritual sex may not even mean that you are attracted to the person that you have sex with, although you could be lusting for them. Mostly it is a powerplay and it means you hate the guy that is married to her, or the girl who is married to that guy. Do you not realize this?

Sleeping with another person's spouse means that you have won, you have conquered them.

So, if you sleep with your father's woman, it says to your father, *I hate you, I am conquering you, I have conquered you.*

Just the same, when you perform illegal sex acts you are cosigning with the devil, saying to the one who gave you the idea, *that's a good idea, I am following you.* That's an initiation for more of the same or for whatever foul act is next in this game of *Do As I Say*.

At the same time, you are sending a hate message to the one who said explicitly in the Bible not to do that. Are you sending hate messages to God, and you are wondering why you are not blessed?

Do you wonder why you are not blessed? Why are you not successful? Why are you not excelling? Why are you not healed? Why are you not any of the things that are written in the Bible that you should be? **We are finding out that it takes stability to have ability.**

Why don't you have the things in the Bible that you know you should have? After all, *it is written*. It didn't change.

You shouldn't wonder; if you are not stable, you won't excel. You are supposed to have those things when you walk in that way.

This is the way, walk ye therein. (Isaiah 30:21)

SO MANY WONDER WHY THEY ARE NOT BLESSED have you entered into the curse of thou shalt not excel by illegal sex? Reuben sent hate messages to his father, Jacob by going up to Jacob's bed.

Folks, we are Jacob, we are *in* Jacob. Jacob couldn't bless Reuben for that very reason. If we are sleeping around, shall we continue to wonder why God who blessed Jacob isn't blessing us?

More Excellent

Reuben, thou art my first born, my might, the beginning of my strength. You are the excellency of my power. That is a tall bill to follow, but it is also a great honor and blessing. Reuben, the heir-apparent--, did he rebel, or did he take it all for granted, as if he could do whatever he wanted and still get the blessing?

God has formed us, blessed us and He is still, by faith calling us His own, His firstborn, His strength. Can we not hear Him say something like, **"In this Earth, you are My son, I have**

begotten you. You are My might, you are My strength, you are My body, My mouthpiece, my eyes and ears and My word in this Earth. You are My strength. You are the excellency of dignity. You should have a more excellent ministry. You are the excellence of power and out of your belly should flow Living Water."

Yes, saints of God, out of our bellies should flow Living Water, not being as unstable water, as in Genesis with Reuben.

Instability is being moved by winds of doctrine and the words of people who may be as wrong as dirt who try to dry you up so you will just be dirt. Salt that has lost its savor, is of no more use than just to be walked on. The person making *suggestions* to you may be sincere, but sincerely wrong, sincerely evil. They may be trying to talk you into what they believe is right or to trick you and they may want to derail you. don't fall for it, know the Word of God for yourself.

Later in 2 Samuel, Absalom, who took the counsel of Ahithophel did the same thing to his father, David, that Reuben had done to Jacob. Ahithophel told Absalom to disrespect his father by sleeping with his father's concubine. This is not just an insult to the person whose woman or women you are hitting on, it is against Levitical Laws provided by God. So, it is sin against God.

Foundational and generational problems? Didn't David also sleep with someone else's wife, and wasn't a woman who used to be someone else's wife, Absalom's mother? It's in the blood, folks. If you saw your father with four wives and they all lived in the same house or compound, wouldn't you think it's an *anything goes* kind of lifestyle? Sons are famous for doing what they see their fathers do, anyway. I'm not defending Reuben, but folks, it is in the blood. Please remember, that Reuben's mother was Leah, and Jacob didn't even love her, so there's that.

Folks: **know** the Word of God and keep your mind stayed on Jesus, on the Word and *in* the Word.

Plots From Hell

When the opposite of what God says is a thought in your head, cast it down; don't act on it.

When you are watching a tv show or a movie and the plot is the OPPOSITE of what God said to do, that is the biggest clue **in** the world that the writer is in the world and *of* the world, and the devil is feeding him plots.

Now if what is on the screen, and you see it or some immature, unsaved, or ignorant person sees it they may think that is a way of life. They may think, *Oh, this is a good idea, I think I'll do that, or be that, or try that--,* and they begin their journey to HELL.

This really happened to me. As an adult, I was talking with an adult guy over some weeks or months. On my own, one night on TV, I saw a stand-up comedian saying some disparaging things about women, in the name of comedy. I thought, this is foul, but if I don't finish watching it, I won't know the scope of this routine or how to address it or judge it. As the programming went on, I thought to myself, if the guy that I am talking to sees this, it will be bad, really bad. I thought, he will believe this.

Sure enough, it happened; this guy changed into a terrible version of himself, and I could feel his hatred toward women because of what a comedian had said. To this day, although we are not in touch, this man probably doesn't know that he changed the day he also watched that *"comedy special."* People, what is broadcast is dangerous to the unsaved, unstable, and those who do not know the Word of God. To this day, this man is unstable--, he goes from job to job, he is unmarried, unsaved, unchurched, and of course does not know the Word of God. He has two children by two women he has never married and never will marry.

Instead of rising to be what God called him to be, he never priested or pastored any home in any Godly way. Whom did he cover in prayer? Whom did he stand watch for? Whom did he intercede for? When it is all said and done, what can he say to the Lord as to how he fulfilled his purpose for being here on the Earth?

Floks, this is instability. This man could have had a completely different life. It would have been best if he had married the woman of his youth that he first impregnated, and they had conceived after marriage, instead of the way it was handled. He is a man of a certain age now. Perhaps we all should look at our lives from the end to the beginning instead of not looking at it at all, or just looking at today not thinking about tomorrow.

For the sake of this man and many more like him, we must do the work of an evangelist, at every turn, since the devil is certainly doing his part to keep people unsaved and drag them to hell.

Unless somebody knows what, any person is thinking or acting out and ministers Jesus to them in time and they repent, they are walking on their way to hell.

Let God Establish You

Humble yourselves therefore under the mighty hand of God, that he may exalt you in due time:

Casting all your care upon him; for he careth for you.

Be sober, be vigilant; because your adversary the devil, as a roaring lion, walketh about, seeking whom he may devour:

Whom resist stedfast in the faith, knowing that the same afflictions are accomplished in your brethren that are in the world.

But the God of all grace, who hath called us unto his eternal glory by Christ Jesus, after that ye have suffered a while, make you perfect, stablish, strengthen, settle you.

To him be glory and dominion for ever and ever. Amen. (1 Peter 5:6-11

The Lord will establish you; that means you will be stable. We want to be stable in our careers, don't we? We want to be stable in our jobs and finances, right? Then stability is a good thing, and we should want to be stable in every aspect of our lives.

Stability requires a real-time relationship with the LORD, not just on Sunday. You can't just not know what to do all week except on Sunday, making that the one day you may go to church and pray. We must have a real time, all the time, 24/7 relationship with the Lord. We don't know what will be thrown at us at any time in this life. Stuff doesn't just come at us on Sunday, although it can. You certainly have seen how many obstacles are keeping you from getting to church, or getting there on time on Sunday, right?

Real time relationship with the Lord via the Holy Spirit is necessary to know what to do in every situation.

- We know the Word of God
- We study the Word of God
- We are covered by the Blood of the LAMB
  We are hearing from God, via the HOLY SPIRIT

Don't Thirst

The water that is in us, since we are 70% water should be the God-kind of water. Out of our bellies should flow Living Water; that Living Water should be in us. Not unstable water as in some weird isotope, some weird water that is not really water. No, Living Water.

We have so many advantages over Reuben and all those in the Old Testament. We have a Better Covenant; we have the Better Blood. We have more Grace ministered to us and available to us. We have power available to us because of the prayers of the Righteous.

Jacob had no way of knowing about this Living Water that Jesus told the woman at the well about. Jacob didn't know that out of the bellies of mere men, people like us, should flow rivers of Living Water and that water would be stable, and we could excel and have the abundant life in this life.

Jacob didn't know that there was water that would never dry up. Neither did he know that those who had that water, those who would receive that water would never thirst again, through Jesus Christ. No, never--, never *thirst* again.

Yet those who believe they have water, but it is the unstable water they continue to THIRST and they in that *thirst* they are thirsting after sexual sin. People, the words that we use as slang are not really slang – read your Bible. Those words and terms are in the Bible. Jesus already said that anyone who gets this Water, will never thirst again. Yet we use that term, *thirst* to say that there are *thirst* traps and there are those who thirst--, that is, strongly desire and chase after sexual sin.

Those are led into sexual sin and once a person commits a sin and they don't repent, they begin to become **UNSTABLE** in their lives and their lives can unravel.

Unfortunately, there are those who treat this life as if it is a toy that God has given them to play with, to amuse themselves with for their 100 years or so, on Earth.

It is not.

Further, on the Cross when Jesus said, *I thirst.,* He meant that as He was losing contact with the Father, that the Living Water in Him would be no more. *I thirst* (John 19:28). Yes, He had lost a lot of blood, but I believe those words were more spiritual than announcing some bodily need, after all, Jesus lived a very fasted life, and His flesh was fully under subjection. Reuben was nothing like Jesus in self-control and flesh control and in his thirst either for carnal pleasure, his hate, or his desire to exert power over his own father, Jacob.

As God's people in the Earth, we should thirst after godliness, and after righteousness, after the Word, and the Presence of God. Our thirst for carnal things should be diminished as we become more like Christ, more stable every day.

… O God, thou *art* my God; early will I seek thee: my soul **thirsteth** for thee, my flesh longeth for thee in a dry and thirsty land, where no water is; (Psalm 63:1)

Repentance

Somewhere in the Jewish volume called the Midrash, it says that Reuben did repent to Moses, and that curse of thou shalt not excel was broken off the tribe of Reuben. Reuben repented when he recognized the error of his ways by defiling his father's bed.

Did we not read that the curse was on the entire Tribe of Reuben, until Reuben repented? Folks, when you sin, you are sinning for yourself and also for your generations.

.   Jacob said on his deathbed, what is usually the blessing:

"Reuben, you art my firstborn, my might, and the beginning of my strength, the excellency of dignity, and the excellency of power: Unstable as water, you shall not excel; because you went up to your father's bed: then you defiled it; he went to my couch."
(Genesis 49:1-4)

But Reuben repented and the curse was broken and forgiven.

THANK GOD FOR REPENTANCE.

There is a message which is just a prayer on the Dr Marlene Miles You Tube channel called *Repentance*. It includes many prayer points for repentance for sexual sins. https://www.youtube.com/watch?v=Ro gSEp2zH9o&t=53s Pray it if you plan to stop fornicating. Pray it if you plan to get into a proper relationship with God, and pray it if you intend to marry the person that God has put into your life.

Repent. Let all the curses be broken. Let all the evil arrows go back to wherever they came from and not hit you and make your life even worse. If it is already unstable or unraveling, you don't need another evil arrow in your life, do you?

I will leave a few prayer points at the end of this chapter, but please know that what is listed here is not nearly the amount of repentance any soul should do. Take the full Repentance prayer on You Tube on my channel; it is far more comprehensive. You may not be a sinner, but my sin is ever before me. I have sinned in this life, and I have Godly sorrow that won't let me forget it. I'm not guilt conscious all the time, but when I think of the goodness and Mercy of God, I am ever thankful because I have sinned.

Take the repentance. Pray the prayers of repentance. Men ought to always repent.

Repent and live.

Repent and excel.

Repent, and be saved.

Whether you want to be **stable** or not, don't play with God by acting on devil influences and ideas and think you can just hide it and get away with it. No, repent. Every idea in your head did not come from you; it is not even your own idea. Every idea in your head did not come from God. Discern. Rightly divide Truth from a lie. Know the Word of God so you don't do the opposite.

AMEN.

Prayer Points

1. Lord, thank You that I am fearfully and wonderfully made, in the Name of Jesus.

2. Thank You, that even though I was conceived in sin and shaped in iniquity, prior to that, You had formed me, but since human hands have touched me and touched my life, I need cleansing and repentance, in the Name of Jesus.

3. Lord forgive me of all my sins and the sins of my ancestors, in the Name of Jesus.

4. Father, forgive my instability, in the Name of Jesus.

5. I bind the *vagabond spirit* that leads me to and fro in this life, in the Name of Jesus.

6. Lord, establish me. Order my steps, light my path, and establish me in the place and relationships that I should be in that I may prosper and bring glory to Your Name.

7. Lord, help me to study and pray, by the Holy Spirit, in the Name of Jesus.

8. Let this mind be in me that was also in Christ Jesus, so that I am not deceived or blow away by winds of doctrine, in the Name of Jesus.

9. Father, after you formed man, after you formed me, You blessed me; let me realize that blessing in my life, in the Name of Jesus.

10. I am the firstborn of Creation, Lord, help me to become a true son of God, in the Name of Jesus.

11. Lord, the things of You that I know, give me

strength and courage to walk in them, no matter what my friends are doing, no matter what my family is saying, in the Name of Jesus.

12. The Godly things I know and believe in, give me fortitude to not waver in that, in the Name of Jesus.

13. Lord, let me not turn my hand back from the plow. Lord, forgive me for any and every time that I ever have, in the Name of Jesus.

14. Lord, make me fit to serve You, in the Name of Jesus.

15. I reject all worldliness; Lord, keep me from being

friends with the world, in the Name of Jesus.

16. Lord, I embrace Your stability and sameness; I trust on You, I rely on You. You are my strong tower, in the Name of Jesus.

17. Tree of the Knowledge of Good and Evil; get out of my life, get out of my eyesight, lose your power to tempt me, in the Name of Jesus.

18. Lord, I renounce and denounce any time that I have bitten from the fruit of that forbidden tree; please forgive me, and cleanse me of all uncleanness and iniquity

by the power in the Blood
of Jesus.

19. Lord, where I have sinned,
forgive me, in the Name of
Jesus.

20. Lord the consequences of
sin to include dullness,
stupidity, being
spellbound and captive,
please heal me, release
me, make me whole again,
in You, in the Name of
Jesus.

21. Holy Spirit, my Helper, be
every with me to give me
sharp discernment, in the
Name of Jesus.

22. Lord, return my glory
where it has been stolen,
or I've lost it or given it

away due to sin, in the Name of Jesus.

23. Make me a shining light for the lost that I may give them Living Water when they ask, and in season, in the Name of Jesus.

24. Lord, forgive me for every time I have not evangelized when I could have or should have. Strengthen me with courage and boldness to be a proper mouthpiece for You in the Earth, in the Name of Jesus.

25. Lord, I set my face like flint, let me never become unstable, in Jesus' Name.

26. Let Living Water ever flow out of my belly, in the Name of Jesus.

27. I thank You, Lord for hearing and answering prayers, know that the answers are already sent, and they are, Yes, and Amen.

28. I seal this Word, these prayers, decrees, declarations, and deliverance across every realm, age, dimension and timeline, past, present, and future, to infinity. I seal them with the Blood of Jesus and also with the Holy Spirit of Promise.

29. Let any backlash planned or executed against these

prayers, this author, any person reading this book and or praying these prayers backfire without mercy against the evil *spirit*, power, agent, or entity to infinity, in the Name of Jesus.

Dear Reader

Thank you for acquiring and reading this book. We are the excellency of God. We are a peculiar treasure to Him. We are called to be priests, and to pastor our own homes. We are His strength in the Earth.

Lord, make us stable, help us to be stable, and remain stable, to the Praise of Your Glory,

In the Name of Jesus,

Amen.

Dr. Marlene Miles

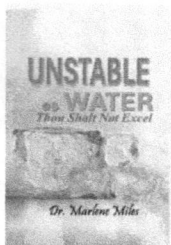

Prayer books by this author

While most books by this author have prayer points either throughout the book or at the end, there are some books that are **only** prayers. You just open up the book and pray. They are listed below:

Prayers Against Barrenness: *For Success in Business and Life*

Fruit of the Womb: *Prayers Against Barrenness*

Beauty Curses, *Warfare Prayers Against*
https://a.co/d/5Xlc20M

Courts of Marriage: Prayers for Marriage in the Courts of Heaven
(prayerbook) https://a.co/d/cNAdgAq

Courtroom Warfare @ Midnight
(prayerbook) https://a.co/d/5fc7Qdp

Demonic Cobwebs *(prayerbook)*
https://a.co/d/fp9Oa2H

Every Evil Bird https://a.co/d/hF1kh1O

Every Evil Arrow
https://a.co/d/afgRkiA

Gates of Thanksgiving

I Call Down Fire (new!)
https://a.co/d/hN7kGnE

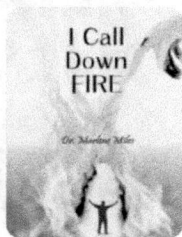

Spirits of Death & the Grave, Pass Over Me and My House
https://a.co/d/dS4ewyr

*Please note that my name is spelled incorrectly on amazon, but not on the book.

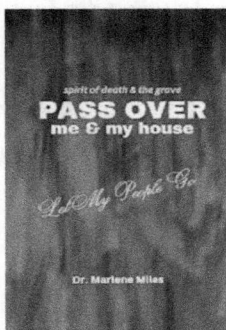

Throne of Grace: Courtroom Prayer

https://a.co/d/fNMxcM9

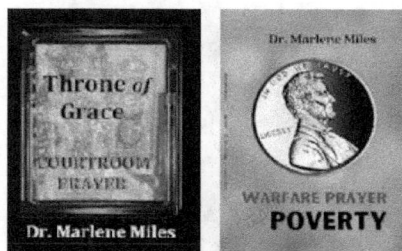

Warfare Prayer Against Poverty
https://a.co/d/bZ611Yu

Other books by this author

AK: *The Adventures of the Agape Kid*

AMONG SOME THIEVES

Ancestral Powers https://a.co/d/9prTyFf

Backstabbers https://a.co/d/gi8iBxf

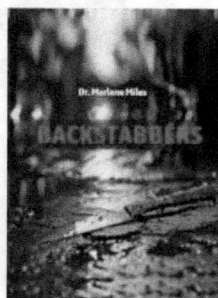

Barrenness, *Prayers Against*
https://a.co/d/feUltIs

Battlefield of Marriage, *The*

Blindsided: *Has the Old Man Bewitched You?* https://a.co/d/5O2fLLR

Break Free from Collective Captivity

Casting Down Imaginations
https://a.co/d/1UxlLqa

Choose An Altar, to Choose A Church

Churchzilla, The Wanna-Be, Supposed-to-be Bride of Christ

Curses of Blind Men

Demonic Cobwebs (prayerbook)

Demonic Time Bombs

Demons Hate Questions

Devil Loves Trauma, *The*

Devil Weapons: Unforgiveness, Bitterness,…

The Devourers: *Thieves of Darkness 2*

Do Not Swear by the Moon

Don't Refuse Me, Lord (4 book series)

https://a.co/d/idP34LG

Dream Defilement

The Emptiers: *Thieves of Darkness, 1*
https://a.co/d/5I4n5mc

Every Evil Arrow
https://a.co/d/afgRkiA

Evil Touch https://a.co/d/gSGGpS1

Failed Assignment
https://a.co/d/3CXtjZY

Fantasy Spirit Spouse
https://a.co/d/hW7oYbX

FAT Demons (The): *Breaking Demonic Curses*

The Fold (5-book series)

- The Fold (Book 1)
- Name Your Seed (Book 2)
- The Poor Attitudes of Money (3)
- Do Not Orphan Your Seed (4)
- For the Sake of the Gospel (5)
- My Sowing Journal

Gang Ups: Touch Not God's Anointed

got HEALING? Verses for Life

got LOVE? Verses for Life

got HOPE? Verses for Life

got money? https://a.co/d/g2av41N

How to Dental Assist

How to Dental Assist2: Be Productive, Not Wasteful

I Take It Back

It's Coming Back: *Vengeance Is the Lord's, So Stop Making Weapons*

Legacy

Let Me Have A Dollar's Worth
https://a.co/d/h8F8XgE

Level the Playing Field

Living for the NOW of God

Lose My Location
https://a.co/d/crD6mV9

Man Safari, *The*

Marriage Ed. Rules of Engagement &
Marriage

Made Perfect in Love

Money Hunters: Beware of Those

Money on the Altar https://a.co/d/4EqJ2Nr

Mulberry Tree https://a.co/d/9nR9rRb

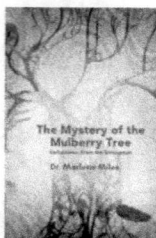

Motherboard (The) - *Soul Prosperity Series*

Name Your Seed

Occupy: *Until I Return*

Plantation Souls

Players Gonna Play

Power Money: Nine Times the Tithe

https://a.co/d/gRt41gy

The Power of Wealth *(forthcoming)*

Powers Above

The Robe, Part 1, The Lessons of Joseph

The Robe, Part II, The Lessons of Joseph

Seasons of Grief

Seasons of Waiting

Seasons of War

Second Marriage, Third--, *Any Marriage*

https://a.co/d/6m6GN4N

Sift You Like Wheat

Six Men Short: What Has Happened to all the Men?

Soul Prosperity soul prosperity series 3

https://a.co/d/5p8YvCN

Souls Captivity soul prosperity series 2

The Spirit of Poverty

StarStruck

SUNBLOCK

The Swallowers: *Thieves of Darkness*, 3

Take It Back

This Is NOT That: How to Keep
Demons from Coming at You

Time Is of the Essence

Too Many Wives: *Why You Have Lady
Problems*

Tormenting Spirits   https://a.co/d/dAogEJf

Toxic Souls

Triangular Power *(series)*

- Powers Above
- SUNBLOCK
- Do Not Swear by the
  Moon
- STARSTRUCK

Uncontested Doom

Unguarded Hours, *The*

Unstable As Water: *Thou Shalt Not Excel*

Unseen Life, *The*

https://a.co/d/0drZ5Ll

Upgrade: How to Get Out of Survival Mode

- Toxic Souls (Book 2 of series)
- Legacy (Book 3 of series)

The Wasters: *Thieves of Darkness*, Bk 2

https://a.co/d/bUvl9Jo

What Have You to Declare? What Do You Have With You from Where You've Been?

When I Was A Child, *I Prayed As a Child*

When the Devourer is Rebuked

https://a.co/d/1HVv8oq

The Wilderness Romance *(series)* This series is about conducting a Godly relationship and marriage with someone who is a Wilderness person. It is about how to recognize it and navigate through it. These books are about how not to get caught up in such.

- *The Social Wilderness*
- *The Sexual Wilderness*
- *The Spiritual Wilderness*

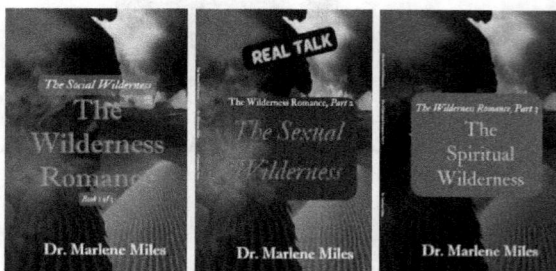

www.ingramcontent.com/pod-product-compliance
Lightning Source LLC
LaVergne TN
LVHW022323080426
835508LV00041B/2320